Foreword by N R Narayana Murthy

ON ENTREPRENEURSHIP AND IMPACT

Desh Deshpande

Table of Contents

☼ Develop

☼ Impact

☼ Engage

Acknowledgements

The book you have in your hand is a collection of some of my reflections on entrepreneurship and social impact. As I wrap up this book, I took a few minutes to reflect on my own entrepreneurial career that started more than three decades ago.

It all started at a small company called ESE in Toronto that was acquired by Motorola in 1980. We moved to Boston in 1984. I was fortunate enough to be involved with several startups some of which included Coral Networks, Cascade Communications, Sycamore Networks, Cimarron, Webdialogs, Airvana, A123 Systems, Tejas Networks and Curata.

This journey brought me in close touch with several mentors, co-founders, colleagues and innovators. They are too many to list individually but I am very thankful to each and every one of them because they have all been a part of my education and have taught me how every entrepreneurial journey is unique, but at the same time share some common themes.

Building a company is very much like a childbirth in many ways. It is an unique experience for every parent and they have to go through the experience to understand the pain and the joy. However, over time the process of childbirth has improved dramatically with better understanding. Similarly, a better understanding of the entrepreneurial

Foreword

In business, you might be able to gain some kind of advantages using shortcuts. These advantages are short-lived. If you want to gain long-term advantage, you need the right foundation of values and principles at play.

"On Entrepreneurship and Impact" is a refreshing take on the themes of entrepreneurship and impact. Every article highlights a value, principle, mindset or an approach at the foundational level rather than providing a popular tip or a technique. The focus is on the long-term win rather than gaining a fleeting advantage.

I have been a witness from close quarters to watch Desh build multiple successful technology companies in the first phase of his career and now repeating his success via thoughtful philanthropy and innovative ecosystem building initiatives like the Sandbox at Hubli and other locations.

In this book, Desh generously shares his practical insights that will create a lasting impact on the thinking of those that are aiming to create a lasting impact.

My advice - read this book in the context of your own projects. Consider putting these insights into action on your own project or share these insights with those that can put them into action.

N R Narayana Murthy
Founder, Infosys
Bangalore
February 2016

When I met Rajesh Setty a couple of years ago I was very impressed by his ability to squeeze concepts down to a few words that get to the essence of the idea. He is an engineer, a serial entrepreneur and a writer. I also work closely with Raj Melville, Executive Director of Deshpande Foundation who is very articulate and gives overall shape to what we do at the Foundation. Together, Rajesh and Raj encouraged me to write this book, something more concise that busy entrepreneurs could read. Without the two of them, this book would not have been written.

I am thankful to Narayana Murty for not only being an excellent role model for entrepreneurship but also writing the foreword to this book. He has not only built a successful company and created opportunities for hundreds of thousands of young Indians, he continues to work on helping the millions of less fortunate Indians who have not been included in the growing economy.

Finally, I want to thank you, the reader. That you picked up this book tells me that you are interested in entrepreneurship, social or otherwise. The world needs more of you to dream big and to work hard to make that dream come true.

Desh
February 2016
Boston, MA

path is improving the entrepreneurial success rate attracting more people to entrepreneurship as a career.

During the last fifteen years, I have spent increasingly more time focused on 'Social Entrepreneurship' starting with the MIT Deshpande Center for Technological Innovation. Slowly, over the course of time our social innovation projects have grown in India, USA and Canada. The people who lead these efforts Leon Sandler, Naveen Jha, David Parker and Karina LeBlanc are entrepreneurs themselves and their commitment is second to none. Their dedicated efforts have produced promising results making my second innings of entrepreneurship so much more meaningful.

My wife Jaishree and my father Shreenivasrao Deshpande have been full participants in this effort and I am thankful for their help and mentorship. My father is uniquely qualified to advise us on this topic because he was born in a small village in India and had a distinguished career that took him to places beyond India. He has seen how people live in villages in India on almost nothing as well as the lifestyles in developed countries.

I have met hundreds of entrepreneurs over the last two decades. In their journey many reach a crossroad where they need to make a decision. What they don't have is time to read big books looking for answers. Several entrepreneurs have thanked me many years later for something I told them in the past. Many of them have asked me to write a book. There are so many books that get published these days that I did not want to add one more to that heap.

Introduction

The world has changed dramatically in the last six decades that I have witnessed. Most of the changes have been brought about by technological innovations and entrepreneurs who have put them to good use. Millions of people have been lifted out of poverty. The power of innovation and entrepreneurship continues to multiply in the connected world we live in.

However, the difference between those who benefit from this new economy and those who get left behind continues to widen. While there is a lot of conversation about a 'shared economy' there is no obvious solution in sight. In some ways entrepreneurship is what is creating this divide. However, I think entrepreneurship can also fix this problem.

Whether it is impoverished pockets in affluent economies or disadvantaged regions in developing countries, the typical approach to addressing the economic divide is by tired approaches that provide handouts, assistance and aid. While these solutions might address the issues in the short term, they seldom stick as there is little local ownership or capacity to absorb them.

We believe that encouraging an entrepreneurial mindset at the grassroots level will better accelerate change and create positive local impact that will eventually lift communities. A clear path to entrepreneurship helps strengthen local ecosystems by providing a hand up to people to fulfil their dreams instead of a handout to continue a basic subsistence,

While we need high tech, fast growth entrepreneurial companies at the high end, we also need to provide people in other segments of society a means to craft their own future through entrepreneurial action. This can only be done by creating a strong ecosystem that highlights local entrepreneurship, identifies and encourages entrepreneurs and builds local economic capacity.

Regardless of the type of entrepreneur, whether a high tech one or at the grassroots level, the challenges and the questions one has to face are similar. This book is targeted at both types. It is an attempt to answer some of the questions that entrepreneurs face. Please reach out to us on the book's website, provide your feedback, ask questions, challenge the issues and ideas. We look forward to publishing a sequel based on your response.

Thank you for being a fellow entrepreneur. Apart from the ability to impact the world, I have found that it is a great way to live. Entrepreneurs share two common attributes; they are naïve and very optimistic. They see every challenge as an opportunity and they believe that tomorrow is always going to be better than today. Nothing can beat living this optimistic life, always hopeful of a better tomorrow. My hope is that millions of optimistic entrepreneurs will take charge of the problems facing their communities, creating a vibrant and more just world where everyone is excited about the future.

START

Are you ready to be an entrepreneur?

The first million-dollar question I want to address is:

Are you ready to be an entrepreneur?

Short answer: You are ready when the only option you see in front of you is that entrepreneurial dream.

Several times at my speaking engagements I get asked different variations of this question like, "I think I have a brilliant idea. Should I start a company?"

My response always is:

"Don't!

Usually, they are not very happy to hear this kind of a response.

Honestly, I am not trying to be blunt when I respond in that fashion.

The reason for their disappointment is because there is a mismatch of expectations.

They are expecting some encouragement, a pep-talk may be.

They are expecting **VALIDATION!**

That rarely works.

If someone is looking for external validation to start

something, there is a really good chance that they are not yet ready. When they are ready, they will know it; they won't need someone else to endorse their quest.

Imagine a kid who got his first bicycle as a present in the evening. He wants to start riding right away. His parents tell him that it's already late and he could ride first thing in the morning. That kid is disappointed. The entire night the kid is tossing and turning in anticipation. He just can't wait for the next morning.

That's the kind of anxious anticipation about launching a company that gets an entrepreneur started.

The keyword that matters most for a first-time entrepreneur: **Conviction!**

Conviction is important because the road ahead is not an easy one. There are going to be problems of all sizes, shapes and colors. You will witness detours, roadblocks and speed bumps more often than you anticipated. Deep conviction is what will keep you going even when you feel like giving up.

Reflect on your quest: Do you have the kind of conviction that will provide the fuel to keep you going the distance?

If yes, you are ready to embark on that entrepreneurial adventure.

If someone is looking for external validation to start something, there is a really good chance that they are not yet ready.

Is entrepreneurship worth it?

Another million-dollar question in the world of entrepreneurship - "Is Entrepreneurship Worth it?

I am sorry to disappoint you if you were expecting a "Yes" or "No" answer for this question.

The Short answer is: **It depends!**

The decision to embark on an entrepreneurial journey is entirely up to you. Only YOU can weigh the pros and cons to see if entrepreneurship is truly worth it.

Having started a few companies AND having closely watched several more entrepreneurial ventures from their inception, I've realized that it all depends on the **fit**.

Entrepreneurship is not, and will never be, easy. It takes time and effort and you never know if you'll taste that elusive success. It takes a certain type of person to cope with that and to move forward.

In some ways entrepreneurship is like playing with fire. Starting a new venture without being ready for it is like sticking your hand in the fire by accident. You get burnt and might be scarred for life. However, if you keep a distance that you are comfortable with, you benefit from the fire's warmth.

Similarly, as a first time entrepreneur you need to find the

right place in the entrepreneurial fire pit. Jump in too soon and unprepared into the thick of things and you might get burnt and never want to try it again. Find the right distance and you will enjoy the experience.

What this means is you need to find the right role as an entrepreneur based on your current capabilities. It might not be playing the lead initially. If you find the right role within an entrepreneurial enterprise, you will enjoy your experience.

The first step to becoming an entrepreneur is knowing yourself and your capabilities.

In closing, I want to share a quote that goes something like this –

"Entrepreneurship is living a few years of life in a way most people won't so that you can live the rest of your life like most people can't."

I don't know who said this, but it is worth reflecting on it as it speaks to the transformational effect an entrepreneurial journey can have on you.

So, here is the real question for you: **Are you up for the challenge?**

 The first step to becoming an entrepreneur is knowing yourself and your capabilities.

Is entrepreneurship an art or a science?

A common question that I have been asked dozens of times is whether entrepreneurship is an art or a science.

I have a feeling that people expect me to choose one or the other, or to say, "It's partly art and it's partly science."

I don't think that is the right answer.

My answer is: "**Entrepreneurship today is no longer an art or science but, a career.**

When we started companies back in the 70's and 80's, there wasn't much of an entrepreneurship culture. If your company failed back then, you would have taken a big hit.

Now, however, we have the infrastructure to make entrepreneurship a full-time career for many around the world. It's perfectly acceptable today to start a second venture, after failing the first, and you might be much better at it the second time around. Some of the biggest entrepreneurs failed at their first company and, as a result, learned a lot of lessons from that initial failure.

Typically, an idea takes 4-6 years to develop. Back in the 70's and 80's, we got one shot at being successful. Today if an idea doesn't work out you can simply start over and try again.

Why is this important?

What it means to be an entrepreneur has changed since my early entrepreneurship days. Today you can make a commitment to entrepreneurship as a career. If you don't feel you are ready to be an entrepreneur, you can still join a small startup to get your feet wet before starting out on your own entrepreneurial journey. You can hone your entrepreneurial skills with experience and practice.

If you want to be an entrepreneur commit yourself to entrepreneurship as a career. Don't look on a single failure as a setback or a blemish on your record but as a learning opportunity to improve yourself and a stepping stone to your next project.

If you want to be an entrepreneur commit yourself to entrepreneurship as a career. Don't look on a single failure as a setback or a blemish on your record but as a learning opportunity to improve yourself and a stepping stone to your next project.

MANAGE

Establishing and communicating a compelling vision

"A leader has the vision and conviction that a dream can be achieved. He inspires the power and energy to get it done."

-Ralph Lauren

Establishing and communicating a compelling vision is very important. It helps you attract great talent, good board members and advisors. It will also move the needle on the investment front.

Doing anything meaningful in life is hard. You need to have a story that explains that while you are setting out to do something hard, it is well WORTH doing.

For example, when we were building Cascade Communications, our vision was very simple.

Just as every phone was connected to every other phone, our vision was to connect every computer to every other computer in the world.

It sounds silly now, but this was 1990 when long distance communications were controlled by monopolies.

To realize our vision, we needed two things:

1) Computer communications networks had to move from private to public networks.

2) The public carriers needed to implement data switches.

Cascade Communications' opportunity was in building packet switches for the public networks.

While building those products we went through a number of iterations and evolved, but the vision remained the same.

Every employee was excited to work on what was on their table. They showed a lot of passion. They obviously knew that their work was contributing to the big vision of connecting all the computers in the world into one network.

One important thing to remember - Setting and communicating a big vision is not the end, but a great beginning.

While there is a need for a big vision, the execution has to be planned step-by-step. A big vision by itself doesn't really change much.

Execution is where the magic happens.

Coming back to the example of Cascade Communications - the journey was not an easy one just because we had a clear and compelling vision. Many venture firms passed on us. Their thinking was that since our buyers were limited to big telecommunication firms, like Verizon and AT&T, a startup like Cascade Communications would be squeezed by these monopolies.

Luckily, timing was on our side. The new regulatory framework in the US gave birth to several smaller players who were eagerly looking for a technology that would provide them with a competitive advantage. The data packet switches from Cascade Communications fit the bill nicely.

In 1997, when the company merged with Ascend Communications and Lucent, Cascade Communications was carrying 80% of the Internet traffic.

I like to build companies where every one of the employees feels like a founder of the company. It is very apparent that they know and believe in the vision when someone asks them, "What do you do?" and you see a spark in their eyes when they answer.

A compelling vision communicated well is what will make your team members excited to come and work Monday morning.

 Doing anything meaningful in life is hard. You need to have a story that explains that while you are setting out to do something hard, it is well WORTH doing.

Three elements of building a winning startup culture

"To win in the marketplace, you have to win in the workplace first"

- Doug Conant, Campbell Soup

Corporate culture is generally defined as the pervasive values, beliefs and attitudes that characterize a company and guide its practices.

While culture operates in an invisible fashion, it's influence in producing results (good and bad) is unquestionable.

Building a winning culture should be a priority for all leaders - irrespective of the size of the company they are leading. If they don't design it well, a culture will get created by default. Most often, the culture that gets created by default is not pretty.

Here are three elements of building a winning startup culture.

1. Egoless:

Let me warn you that this is easier said than done. You have to create an environment where ideas don't have authorship and people love solving problems without worrying about who solved the problems. In reality, we all know that it takes more than one person to solve a problem. This kind of a mindset will automatically make the work environment fun and rewarding.

A side benefit of this is that nobody will continue to defend and pursue a mediocre idea.

2. Cohesive:

A startup is like a team of people in a canoe. A canoe moves and gains speed only when everyone is working in cohesion.

Granted, this involves making certain compromises such as striking the right balance between "quality" and "time to market." Once a decision has been made whether everyone fully buys into it or not, they have to support the team. Without cohesion, there will be lot of activity, but not much productivity. Following the canoe analogy, without everyone rowing in the same direction, the canoe simply treads water and never gains speed.

3. Listening

It is common for startups to change direction based on marketplace feedback. This feedback can come from customers or prospects or from one or more initiatives from the competition. You can change direction ONLY if you and your team are "listening" to feedback without being biased. You will face an uphill task in making progress if you are not open and willing to change in the face of feedback.

Most importantly, leaders have to set the right tone for the culture with their actions instead of simply talking about the need for a better culture.

 Building a winning culture should be a priority for all leaders - irrespective of the size of the company they are leading.

How do you delegate effectively?

"If you want to go fast, go alone.
If you want to go far, go together"

- *African Proverb*

Delegation is not easy.

You want to delegate, but you feel that the other person may not do that job as well as you can do it. So, you hesitate.

On the other hand, you also know that without delegating, you are limited by your capacity to get things done.

Here are three elements to help you effectively delegate.

The first key element here is **trust**. Without trust, delegation is almost impossible.

I have a binary relationship when it comes to trust.

Either I trust someone or I don't.

If I don't trust someone, the option becomes simple – I fire that person.

If I trust someone, then I will work with that person, give them the creative freedom and also help them grow and become more effective.

The second key element is **effective communication**.

You have a clear idea of what needs to get done. The person you are delegating the task to initially has zero idea. The more clearly you can communicate your expectations for the task, the better the outcome. If the other person has to do a lot of guesswork, they most likely will do so and the result may not be what you are expecting.

The third key element is **alignment of strengths**.

You are delegating a task to increase your own capacity to get things done and not to test the other person on their skills and strengths.

If the delegated task is not in the area of the other person's strengths, there is bound to be frustration for both parties.

On the other hand, if the delegated task is in the area of the other person's strengths, it's a pleasure for both parties.

You should ensure that there is an alignment of strengths based on the person's past accomplishments, their interests and your history with them.

In summary, delegation is the key to scale. If you delegate a task by clearly communicating the expected outcome to a trusted person and ensure that the task is aligned with their strengths, you have a win-win situation.

Delegation is the key to scale. If you delegate a task by clearly communicating the expected outcome to a trusted person and ensure that the task is aligned with their strengths, you have a win-win situation.

How do you handle difficult conversations in your startup?

"Fierce conversations are about moral courage, clear requests and taking actions"

- Susan Scott, Fierce Conversations

There are numerous stories of startups that started with a wonderful idea, great promise, initial traction and were soon biting the dust - not because the marketplace demand diminished - but because of conflicts between founders or key leaders in the company.

In short: There is harmony when every key player in a startup is wedded to the company mission. There is conflict when key players depart from the core mission.

Conflict happens in startups.

It happens more often than we imagine, because not all conflicts come to light.

How you handle conflicts as a leader will make a big difference as to where your startup is headed and, more importantly, how fast it's headed in that direction.

Let's take the extreme case where one of the key players has a change of heart for the worse (as it relates to the startup, of course). They were passionate about the idea and the mission, but something happened and they have lost interest.

What do you do?

You should have a frank and fair discussion and respectfully ask them to leave. Wish them well with their future. It is the right thing to do, both for their sake and for the sake of those that remain with the company.

This seems hard to do, but not taking this step and maintaining the status quo would be more painful.

Now, let me address a situation that is a bit more complex.

One of the founders has a different take on how things should progress. They have a strong opinion about changing the core company mission. In short, you both have a difference of opinion the size of the Grand Canyon - a difference you can't ignore.

This is the time to have a mature, or as Susan Scott puts it - a fierce conversation.

While there is no guarantee that either of you are right or wrong, it is important for both of you to leave your ego at the door so you both can have an objective take on the issue at hand.

At the end, if you feel that the other person is right, you will be better served by accepting their assessment and making the necessary changes. You are not showcasing your weakness if you change direction. In fact, you are demonstrating strength and openness to listening to sound advice. You will deepen and extend their loyalty for a long time to come.

On the other hand, if you are right, but unable to convince the other person to see your point of view, you are back to square one. It will be better for them to leave rather than making it hard for both of you. You both want the best for the company and a radical step like this is sometimes necessary.

I remember my first venture that I co-founded. It took one year to get funded. A few months after funding, it was clear that my co-founder and I had irreconcilable differences of opinion on how we should proceed.

Long story short, I walked out of the company even though my personal situation was not that great. It was painful when I took that decision. Looking back, it was the best decision I made.

In short, facing reality is painful in the short-term. However, not facing it head on could be detrimental for you and the company in the long-term.

Facing reality is painful in the short-term. However, not facing it head on could be detrimental for you and the company in the long-term.

How does an entrepreneur bounce back from failure?

"Failure is simply the opportunity to begin again, this time more intelligently"

- Henry Ford

It is common knowledge that failure is part and parcel of an entrepreneur's life.

If you have never failed, then there is a possibility that you never tried to do anything that was on the edge.

Broadly speaking, there are two kinds of failures:

a) You failed because of external circumstances on which you had limited control

b) You failed because of your own flawed assumptions, decisions or actions.

In both the cases, the consequences of failure may be the same. For example, you might suffer a financial loss, emotional pain and, sometimes, even strained relationships.

However, the way you approach failure is very different for each case.

Let me explain.

a) Failing due to external circumstances beyond your control

This should rarely shatter you. This kind of failure happens and is more common than you can imagine. As I said before, it hurts no matter what, but for this case recovery should be quick and fast. If you explain what really happened, people understand and will be supportive of your next adventure.

In my first startup adventure, I quit in the middle when I failed to convince my partner, Frank, that going to market quickly was more important than building all the features that we had been planning. Although the product that I wanted to release was head and shoulders above the available alternatives, Frank was of the opinion that we needed a lot more features.

We clearly had a strong difference of opinion.

I quit and in the eyes of the society, I had failed.

The consequences and the pain was real.

Internally, it didn't affect me much as I felt that I did the absolute right thing.

I recovered quickly and was able to raise venture capital for my next startup in the coming months.

b) Failing because of you

When this happens, you clearly know YOU were the reason for that failure.

The first step is to acknowledge that fact and try not to blame it on something external.

The second step is to take the time to pause and reflect on what you could learn from this failure and actually make the necessary changes so that you become better the next time around. This requires a level of humility that is not very common. It is easier to get away by blaming something or someone.

The last step is to consciously rekindle the fire that started you on the entrepreneurial path in the first place.

Any kind of failure rarely shuts the entrepreneurial door permanently, unless you allow it to do so. Use your failures as stepping stones to emerge as a better-equipped person to take on the next adventure.

Use your failures as stepping stones to emerge as a better-equipped person to take on the next adventure.

How to avoid making bad decisions or mistakes in your startup?

Entrepreneurs ask me, "Desh, how do I avoid making mistakes or bad decisions that could hurt my startup?"

This is a two-part question about a) avoiding bad decisions and b) avoiding making mistakes.

On Bad Decisions: People think they have made a bad decision in retrospect. When they are about to make a decision in a fast-paced environment, they are always making the 'right' decision based on all the facts available at that time.

On Mistakes: Mistakes are ideas that people hang onto even when they know it is not a good idea.

In a dynamic startup environment, you might make 10 decisions a week. All of those decisions seem like good ones at the moment, because you obviously wouldn't do it if it wasn't in the best interest of the company.

Whether those decisions are right or wrong only becomes clear with time when you realize that some of those decisions were beneficial to your company and some weren't. Looking back, some of those decisions now appear like bad decisions.

Great leaders create value for their organization as they are able to weed out bad decisions and to stop investing resources in those areas right away.

Ego plays a big role.

There are two types of ego: personal ego and organizational ego.

In egocentric organizations, there's a focus on "authorship of ideas". Employees know who has come up with the idea and people take pride in their contribution. When something doesn't work the strong association with the idea makes it harder for an employee to let go. The decisions become personal, political and emotional.

In egoless organizations where people are really excited about thinking through and coming up with solutions, "authorship of ideas" disappears. The team looks at an idea objectively and together, instead of bringing individual egos into the picture. If it becomes obvious that an idea isn't a good one, the team quickly comes to a consensus that it shouldn't be done and moves on. It's a much better way of working with others. The sole focus is the wellbeing of the company and not the individual.

It's hard for anyone to operate in ideal conditions where there are no mistakes, no ego and all the right decisions. However, being humble and being aware of times when your ego is taking over will help you smoothen the ride.

In closing, the key to avoiding bad decisions is to manage your ego.

 The key to avoiding bad decisions is to manage your ego.

GROW

How do you establish a unique competitive advantage for your startup?

Every startup that wants to become an industry leader loves to have one thing: **a unique competitive advantage.**

So, the question therefore - How do new startups go about establishing that for themselves?

A competitive advantage, particularly a unique one, happens because you see something in the marketplace that others don't.

There are three determinants that help you create a competitive advantage.

The first is a disruptive new technology or approach that you can apply in your sector to create a significant change. For example, with advances in lasers it became easier to use them to modulate data. At Sycamore, we were able to drastically increase the speed of transmission from megabits to gigabits by applying these advances to the field of telecommunications.

The second is to have a vision that is unique, but achievable. In the 1990s, we envisioned a future where every computer in the world would be connected in a network. That sounds silly now but was not the case then.

We believed that just as telephones evolved from individual private networks to a national switched network over the past fifty years, so would computers in the future. That was the premise of Cascade Communications which turned out to be hugely successful.

Which leads to the third premise – you perceive an opportunity that is not obvious to the market leaders. As Clayton Christensen pointed out in his seminal work, **disruptive innovation typically tends to be produced by outsiders**. The entrenched market leaders are focused on their current technology and markets. Even if they see new technologies, they are usually unwilling to make major changes to their product and are satisfied with incremental change. New entrants on the other hand have a blank slate to work with. This enables them to create products that are significantly faster, better or cheaper than what was possible.

Finally, **executing well and moving fast to establish yourself as a leader in the market** and maintaining your market share helps maintain that competitive advantage. By being a dominant player you have a better understanding of a wide range of customer needs and greater knowledge of the market that you can use competitively to further your position.

How to stay ahead of your competition?

"The wise learn many things from their enemies"

- Aristophanes

Remember that having a unique competitive advantage does not mean that you have eliminated the competition.

Dealing with competition is sort of a dilemma for startup entrepreneurs.

On one hand, worrying about competition is meaningless when you don't have anything meaningful to offer to the marketplace.

On the other hand, understanding what the competition is doing is extremely useful as you are responsible to bring out a meaningfully differentiated product to the marketplace.

I am going to focus on the latter for the rest of this article.

It is rare for a startup to come up with an offer that has never existed in the marketplace because not only is it risky, but "lack of demand" may be the real reason such an offer has not existed before.

In other words, when you are starting out, there is a good chance that there are established players in the space that are offering something similar to what you are planning to do. If you offer exactly what the incumbents (your competition) are offering, your sole option is to compete on price which is rarely an advantage for a startup with limited resources.

So, what else can you do?

You have to focus on meaningful differentiation - how your product is positioned, a lower cost design, the way it is distributed, ease of use etc.

For you to clearly differentiate your product, you need to understand the competition well and also validate that your product differentiation will be valued by your target customers.

Along the way, your competitors will come up with all sorts of offerings and upgrades. Your response should be to go back to the drawing board and revisit why you decided to start the company in the first place AND whether your assumptions related to meaningful differentiation are still valid. If both items check out, your next step should be a heads down focus on execution.

In the early days of our company Cascade Communications, telecommunications networks were primarily built for phones. Cascade was focused on building equipment to build public networks for data. All the large telecommunications vendors saw the opportunity but they addressed the market tangentially; they sold large phone switches for millions of dollars and then added a little bit of data syrup on it to handle data. Since Cascade was focussed on data primarily it was able to design data switches that were an order of magnitude less costly and more capable of handling the volume of traffic. The differentiation was very clear and allowed the company to focus on execution and not get distracted by the announcements being made by competitors.

In closing, it's never about ignoring your competition. It is about acknowledging it exists, but sticking to your core meaningfully differentiated offering with a relentless focus on execution.

It's never about ignoring your competition. It is about acknowledging it exists, but sticking to your core meaningfully differentiated offering with a relentless focus on execution.

Three key characteristics of entrepreneurs that can build companies that scale

"Intelligence without ambition is a bird without wings."

- Salvador Dali

"What enables entrepreneurs to build scalable companies?"

An enterprise that scales is an exception rather than a rule.

There are a few characteristics that need to come together in an entrepreneur for them to be successful in scaling their idea into a significant company.

The first is the right blend of managerial **skills**. Entrepreneurs need to know how to manage growth, to delegate effectively and motivate people as their companies grow.

However management skills alone are not sufficient unless they also possess a certain desire, a certain **ambition**. An entrepreneur's ambition has to be big in order to be able to build a large company. The size of your ambition will ultimately affect your vision, as well as how you set goals.

In addition, your **implicit expectations** are also the limiting factor in your goal setting. For example, if your goal is for personal financial independence, you might seize an opportunity for an exit sooner as it might allow you to build your nest egg before your company reaches its full potential.

That brings me to the last and equally important element: **commitment**. I often like to compare this to swimming. If you are practicing, and set a goal of 50 laps a day, the early laps might go great, but then as you approach the fiftieth lap the going gets harder. It is only with commitment that you will finish and achieve that goal.

Yes, building a large company does require many other skills, as you will have to do many different tasks, but if you aren't committed, the company will only go as far as you take it.

No doubt as an entrepreneur, there will be many challenges along your journey. It's that **ambition** to make a meaningful difference in the world and the **commitment** to keep going against all odds that will get you to the destination and beyond!

How should entrepreneurs approach the valuation question?

First, remember that valuation is subjective.

It depends on variety of factors, the three basic ones are:

a) Who you are and what are your past accomplishments?

b) Who are the investors (eg: friends and family, angels, venture capitalists)?

c) What is the nature of the opportunity?

Let's talk about the first factor – who you are and your entrepreneurial accomplishments to date.

The rules are different for someone who has returned hundreds of millions of dollars to investors versus a first-time entrepreneur.

It is not uncommon for one startup to be valued at $2M and another similar-stage startup to be valued at $500M – the difference being the former was led by a first-time entrepreneur and the latter was led by an extremely successful serial entrepreneur.

Entrepreneurship is a risky game and the odds of a first-time entrepreneur winning this game are very low. Super successful serial entrepreneurs provide the social proof that they have better odds of winning the game. Hence they command a premium in valuation.

Let's look at the second factor – who are the investors?

Friends and family members invest mainly to support you and seldom do a full-blown due diligence on the opportunity at hand.

Angel investors are more sophisticated than friends and family. They are excited about you and the opportunity you present. However, they are less demanding when it comes to valuation.

On the other hand, venture capitalists (VCs), have mandates about how to deploy their capital and under what terms. They have to answer to the limited partners and get the returns promised to them or else risk losing their ability to raise the next fund.

For instance, VCs generally want to own a certain percentage of the company in which they are investing. They are more concerned with their ownership stake than the capital invested.

In this case, the valuation is based on the ownership stake the VC is aiming for in the venture.

The last factor that might change the valuation equation is the nature of the opportunity.

Imagine that you bootstrapped a venture that resonated with the market brilliantly. Your venture is growing rapidly through word-of-mouth and your cost of acquiring new customers is very low.

Irrespective of who you are, it is clear that this opportunity is very compelling for investors. Multiple investors start wooing you creating a healthy competition for a share of your business and ultimately boosting your valuation.

In summary, the analogy I like to give is that of selling a home. The price you can ask for a home is what the market is willing to pay. A startup valuation is no different.

Focus on building a startup that is valuable and the valuation will automatically take care of itself.

Focus on building a startup that is valuable and the valuation will automatically take care of itself.

How do you select the right board members for your startup?

The right board plays a key role in any startup.

Board members jointly oversee the activities of a company or organization, and help the leader make the right decisions on major issues.

How does an entrepreneur go about selecting the right members for her board?

Let's dig a bit deeper into this issue.

Entrepreneurs need good board members to help grow their companies.

You won't be an exception.

You need good board members for various reasons. A couple of important ones are:

- They help you think through the problems and brainstorm solutions

- They provide the focus that is very crucial at all stages of the company.

At the foundational level, you want help from people who have done it before.

Board members who haven't "been there, done that" suffer from two key problems:

- They don't quite realize how limited a startup's resources are, and, therefore, don't realize how important "focus" is in order to succeed. Instead of narrowing the company's focus, they tend to want to look at all the possibilities that the company can do. They may come across as smart, but at the expense of adding more work for the company.

- Sometimes they are frustrated entrepreneurs. They have a deep desire to do things, but haven't done them yet. They start to practice their entrepreneurship through your company. Instead of letting you run your company, they think they are helping by getting involved in all the details.

A board member should be there to ask you tough questions, and to give you comfort that you are heading the right way.

Personally, I have transitioned from a life as an entrepreneur to one as a board member. In most cases, whenever an entrepreneur comes to me with a problem, I just turn it back to them and ask, "If you were me, how would you address this issue?" Ninety-nine percent of the time the entrepreneur has a better answer than anything I could have told her.

The main thing the entrepreneur is looking for is external validation, that someone else agrees with their particular decision. A lot of times, a key role for a board member is to be a mentor to the entrepreneur.

The role of a board member is a little bit like the role of a parent teaching a child to walk for the first time. You want to make sure that the child doesn't fall off a staircase, but you also don't want to chide the child for tripping on the carpet.

Having the right board members will amplify your capacity to execute. On the other hand, picking the wrong ones will cost you dearly down the road.

When should an entrepreneur exit from a venture?

Entrepreneurs often ask me, "Should I start a company now?"

My answer to them always is "No!"

Entrepreneurs who have a firm conviction about their new venture do not need external validation.

Similarly, entrepreneurs who are firmly convinced of the value their company is creating and who are focused on building their organization, capturing new customers, enhancing the customer experience and providing enriched value for their stakeholders, don't see planning for an exit as a priority. They are convinced their company is providing a critical resource that the world needs.

At some stage during a company's growth the entrepreneur starts focusing on managing risks. Whether it is from competition or changing markets or other fronts, risk mitigation begins to dominate their thinking. The job that was once all about managing exciting growth becomes one of managing risk.

It is at times like these that manager's start thinking of exits. That inflection point can happen anytime and depends on the personality of the entrepreneur.

I have known entrepreneurs who have built very large companies. They were so confident of the future potential value they could create that the risks seemed insignificant in comparison. They reset their growth goals repeatedly. When $100 million seemed achievable, they raised it to $250 million. As $250 million approached they reached for $1 billion. An exit was the last thing on their mind.

On the other hand, some entrepreneurs start to worry about things when they are still small. If you spend your time worrying more about the risk factors than the growth opportunities, it is a sign that you should be thinking of an exit, either personally or for the company.

Of course there are extreme situations when companies might be on life support due to factors beyond their control or otherwise. In that case you have no choice but to come up with an exit strategy.

If you spend your time worrying more about the risk factors than the growth opportunities, it is a sign that you should be thinking of an exit, either personally or for the company.

DEVELOP

Building an entrepreneurial ecosystem

I have found that there are three types of people in this world; some are oblivious to everything around them, some see problems and complain about them and some see problems and get all excited about solving them. The difference between a vibrant community and an impoverished community is the mix of the second and third type of people. When I look at places like Silicon Valley and Cambridge, Massachusetts they are filled with folks who are looking to solve problems. In fact, entrepreneurship is so widespread that entrepreneurs typically struggle to find meaningful problems to solve.

In impoverished communities, whether they are in affluent economies or developing countries, a large part of the community tends to sit around and complain. This is because they their problems have become chronic and not easily solvable. As a result, they feel victimized and their every conversation quickly turns into complaining about everything. They expect others to solve the problems due to their feeling of helplessness.

The typical approach to this situation has been to bring in external help. Either the government or the philanthropic community come in and often study the overall situation, pick the most important problems and try to come up with a solution. Unfortunately, most of them fail because there is a no local ownership. When the intervention is over and the outsiders leave, things revert back.

For the last ten years, we have been trying a different approach with some success. Instead of solving the problems, we try to identify and encourage problem solvers independent of which problem they want to solve. This has two benefits; the solutions they come up with tend to be very relevant to the local situation and by strengthening local resources it becomes easy to build the capacity to spread the solution.

As you build this local capacity, as more people become problem solvers, they are able to absorb bigger ideas from the outside and execute them.

We have seen this situation evolve in India. We started the 'Social Innovation Sandbox' project in Hubli, India about 9 years ago. Over the years the team, built from local resources, has strengthened their capabilities and improved their self-confidence to the point that they can now engage with the teams from advanced institutions like the Massachusetts Institute of Technology (MIT) on a peer to peer basis.

By building local capacity and creating more problem solvers, the region benefits from their solutions. More importantly, as they grow in capability, they provide a fertile opportunity to seed new ideas from outside and guarantee their growth and adoption.

Partnering with outside organizations becomes easier as the local resources serve as a bridge that provides better understanding and requirements to partners like MIT, while allowing the partners to test and implement their solutions with confidence in local resources. The result is a win-win situation where the local ecosystem grows while providing and accessing solutions that it might not have had otherwise.

My hope is that we can continue to understand this dynamic so that we can effectively innovate globally and execute locally scalable solutions that the world has not seen before.

The one mistake entrepreneurs should avoid

A question often asked is - "What is the most common mistake entrepreneurs make?"

When I reflected on this question, I could think of several mistakes most of us have made at some point as entrepreneurs but the ONE thing that most entrepreneurs need to be careful about is:

Trying to do too much.

Entrepreneurs don't lack commitment. Most entrepreneurs are very committed. The problem is they sometimes commit to too many things.

Let me double-click on this a little bit...

I've noticed that a lot of people are getting into entrepreneurship because they think it's easy. The media is partly to blame for this. When someone reads a "rags to riches" story of entrepreneurs who have made it happen, it is bound to make a wantrepreneur think entrepreneurship must be easy. This is the wrong mindset to have, as you end up adding more to your plate than you can handle.

Entrepreneurship in general gets more complex every step of the way. As you start to tackle the tasks that you've taken on, there will always be a need for more resources, more time, and more money. This is a new feeling for a first time entrepreneur. When an entrepreneur runs out of resources the company ultimately fails.

How can you avoid this?

New entrepreneurs need to figure out how to match the amount of resources to the problem they are trying to solve. If the problem is under-resourced, you are guaranteed to fail due to...yes, you guessed it right - **the lack of resources**.

Another important tip for new entrepreneurs is that you need to find your market. If customers come to you and say, "I'll buy your product if you had X", then you haven't yet found your market. This also leads to the "trying to do too much" problem, because you end up trying to appease all of the customers by adding in the many different requested features.

Don't confuse this with pivoting. It's completely acceptable to pivot. If your company does "A", and 10 people say you should be doing "B", then it's completely fine to pivot and stop doing "A", and focus on "B". The problem occurs when you try to do "A", "B", "C", and "D", and you don't have the resources to test the marketplace for all the features. It's completely fine to change if many people request the SAME thing, but if you find yourself pulled in different directions to add 10 different things, then you have not yet focused your company on a viable product and market. You may need to further refine your idea or find another area where you can effectively serve your target customer and find your place as a company.

I want to leave you with one final piece of advice: **don't hedge your bets by trying too many things.** As a small startup you need to be laser focused on your main value proposition. Big companies can afford to hedge their bets as they have the resources to do so. With limited resources, small startups should only focus on THE area that provides value and should not spread their limited resources too thinly over multiple areas.

In summary, if you really want to be an entrepreneur, don't burn yourself out by doing too much at once. Focus on the most appropriate problem with the resources available to you, and magic will happen

Entrepreneurs don't lack commitment. Most entrepreneurs are very committed. The problem is they sometimes commit to too many things.

How to keep your focus against all odds?

"The ones who are crazy enough to think they can change the world, are the ones who do."

- Steve Jobs

People ask me all the time, "Desh, the people around me have lost faith and given up on my idea, but I continue to believe in it. I see a need for my company in the market, but the others around me don't. How should I handle this situation?"

I think it boils down to a very simple question:

Do you really believe in what you set out to accomplish?

If you doubt yourself, and are doing it for the sake of your ego, then it's not a good way to run a company.

If you believe in your idea, you do so for a reason. Go back to the source and reclaim that power to get motivated to stay the course.

The game of entrepreneurship has changed tremendously from when I started. Back then, if you wanted to start a company, it was usually in isolation, but now, it's seen as a career. Nowadays, if things go wrong, the entrepreneur has many options, including changing the business model or pivoting, to name a few.

In 1990, I started a company called Cascade Communications, and in our first year, we had 12 engineers. I would often invite people I knew in the industry to come in and talk to our employees. They would often tell us our company wouldn't work, because of the limited view they had. Since we had so much more insight into the problem that we were trying to solve and because we spent a significant amount of time on solving that problem, we didn't listen to them.

There are usually one or two reasons for why a company will work, but around fifty reasons as to why it will not. Cascade Communications was no exception. Most of the objections raised were irrelevant, because we knew the technology had moved around, and our approach and solution were both practical and relevant. However, we did think through the other possible objections before moving forward. The objections raised helped us to strengthen our product offering and, more importantly, it strengthened our resolve to continue going after our dream.

My point is that entrepreneurs shouldn't listen to every single piece of criticism coming their way, as they will end up spending too much time trying to satiate everyone. However, if you start to see a recurring pattern in the criticisms, it might be time to reevaluate what you are doing in the market.

It's important for entrepreneurs to find that balance, where they still keep their passion alive, but also keep their ears open to any sort of patterns in the criticism that come their way.

In summary, as long as you believe your company will fulfil a pressing need in the world, it will keep you going in the tough times.

If you believe in your idea, you do so for a reason. Go back to the source and reclaim that power to get motivated to stay the course.

How to make the most of mentors in a startup?

"The greatest good you can do for another is not just to share your riches, but to reveal to him his own."

- Benjamin Disraeli

Mentoring is an interesting topic.

Most entrepreneurs look for mentors at the wrong time. They look for help when they are facing a tactical problem and are already in trouble.

Though they go to someone with a mentoring request, their immediate need is for a purchase order or a capital investment.

The problem?

They will get neither a capital investment nor a purchase order

Free consulting requests should not be disguised as mentoring requests.

The other problem I see is that entrepreneurs pursue famous people as their mentors. This rarely works for two reasons (1) famous people have many other demands for their time

---

and many of those other requests may be more attractive to them and (2) they just don't have the bandwidth to pay attention.

A better approach is to engage with mentors to sharpen your thinking. Find and engage a mentor if you want to bounce off your ideas, get an alternate perspective or look for a second opinion.

Sometimes when an entrepreneur comes to me for advice, I turn the question back to them,

"If you were me, what would you do in this situation?"

Not surprisingly, in most cases entrepreneurs have brilliant answers to their own questions.

They have it within them.

Why do they go to someone else looking for answers?

Because they want to be sure.

Because they have not done this before.

And, most importantly, because they trust the mentor to provide sound advice without bias.

Three things to remember when it comes to mentoring:

It's about chemistry: Before you embark on a journey with your mentor, check if there is chemistry between the two of you. Without the right chemistry, the relationship will be short-lived, even if there is enormous value being added.

It's about timing: Sometimes it's all about the timing. You might catch the right potential mentor, but at the wrong time. You will get a "No" for your request. The "No" is not about you - it's about them not having time for someone then. Don't read between the lines and take that rejection personally.

It's about expectations: As I mentioned before, you need to get your agenda with the mentor right. Your mentoring request should not be your indirect attempt to land funding or a customer deal. While on this topic of expectations, make sure that engaging with you is rewarding for the mentor as well.

On maintaining work and life balance

"There is no such thing as work-life balance. There are work-life choices, and you make them, and they have consequences."

- Jack Welch

Entrepreneurs often come to me with this dilemma - "If I focus too much on my work, I lose touch with the other parts of my life, like family, but if I don't focus, I'm afraid I might not get much done. How do I find the balance between the two extremes?"

My answer boils down to one statement:

Simplify your life!

What does that mean?

You have to be very clear on what your priorities are.

They can't be more than two or three things.

Otherwise, you are doing too much.

During my startup days, I had only two key priorities a) my startup and b) my family. I deliberately refrained from activities that my friends were involved in; like playing golf, family vacations or going to the movies.

So many smart people fall into a trap where they do a hundred different things and justify it all by relating it back to their priority number one. For example, when running a company, even a few silly decisions you make could be justified by saying that it's important for the company. All that does is create more activities, most of them meaningless in the long run.

Clear thinking and clear priorities is the path forward towards maintaining balance.

I heard this quote a few years ago and it resonated with me a lot:

> "Imagine life as a game in which you are juggling some five balls in the air. You name them – Work, Family, Health, Friends and Spirit and you're keeping all of these in the air.
>
> You will soon understand that work is a rubber ball. If you drop it, it will bounce back. But the other four balls – Family, Health, Friends and Spirit – are made of glass. If you drop one of these; they will be irrevocably scuffed, marked, nicked, damaged or even shattered. They will never be the same. You must understand that and strive for it.
>
> Work efficiently during office hours and leave on time. Give the required time to your family, friends and have proper rest. Value has a value only if its value is valued."
>
> *- Bryan Dyson, former CEO of Coca Cola*

A lot of people make mistakes in this area of their life. I personally know many successful people who don't spend enough time with their family or kids and are left with only the rubber ball after a meaningless success.

In order for you to be able to manage your responsibilities and maintain that balance, it will take effort, but it's worth it in the end.

 Clear thinking and clear priorities is the path forward towards maintaining balance.

IMPACT

What are the two big challenges for a Social Impact project?

Evaluating an early stage idea for a social impact project is different than a for-profit enterprise.

The first part is **relevance**.

In the case of technological innovation, you always start with some idea the world has never seen before. This idea will not have an impact on the world unless it addresses a burning problem.

The formula for technological innovation is:

Innovation + Relevance = Impact

The Deshpande Center at the MIT finds relevance to ideas that the world has not known before.

When it comes to social innovation, it is the other way round. The formula goes something like this:

Relevance + Innovation = Impact

Here, the most important thing is a deep understanding of the social issue itself. That is the core competency. You then bring whatever new ideas are needed to solve that problem. Those ideas don't have to be patentable, technically brilliant or provide a huge competitive advantage.

The second part that's equally important is **distribution capability**.

In the for-profit context, the distribution models are relatively clear with typically well-established channels available for most products.

In the case of a social impact project, you have to rely on "insiders" within the community that you are targeting to help distribute your solution. You need to find passionate, committed people who are interested and willing to go the last mile to implement the solution that you are creating.

Without this distribution model, chances are high that your idea will face infant mortality however attractive it might sound on paper.

The passionate, committed group of people may need to be trained as they may not have all the talent and capabilities to immediately execute your plan. You need to factor in this investment in preparing the local resources if you want to have a successful implementation.

By finding the passionate, committed group of people from within the impacted community who can help distribute your solution, will also help address the issue of relevance as they will bring a deeper understanding of local issues.

In summary, you will have successful social impact if it is relevant and you can find and train passionate, committed people from the local communities that can help execute your idea.

What is the best way to start thinking about social impact?

Our world has been blessed with fantastic thinkers and innovators. Luckily, many among them also are hungry to make a meaningful and long-lasting impact for the betterment of this world.

What I've found over the last fifteen years is that it's not enough to come up with a fantastic idea and take that intervention to the people who need it.

The solution often fails after the entrepreneur or innovator has put his or her heart into developing it.

There are many reasons for these failures but ignoring two key principles might be the root of many of the problems

• Designing solutions appropriate to the locale

• Building a viable business model

Let me elaborate on each of these in detail.

As I have mentioned previously, Relevance is a key issue when designing solutions for social impact. Too often the solutions are proposed by practitioners who have a superficial understanding of the local conditions and context. From a personal perspective, they might not even share a common lifestyle with the potential beneficiaries. In many cases they lead with a technical solution.

The other aspect is developing a robust implementation and business model. This does not automatically imply a for profit solution. Instead it is a need for a well thought out approach to both distributing the solution as well as ensuring sustainability. Too often there is an eagerness to target the end customer as the potential user of the solution when in actuality it might be appropriate to target an intermediate level of user who might derive more value. This colors both the product requirements by sometimes making them a lot more rigorous than required as well as the economic model by often targeting a much more unrealistically low price point.

Let me illustrate with an example that was the result of a relationship with MIT and our Hubli Sandbox.

> Recently a team of researchers from MIT visited the Hubli Sandbox. The MIT researchers' goal was to figure out how to help the majority of Indian farmers who generally have small land holdings of a few acres. Most of the technology developed in the West was for farmers with large land holdings.

> With the help of the Hubli team, they spent two weeks with the farmers holding in-depth focus sessions where they figured out a critical need for these farmers.

> It was Soil testing!

Soil testing right now is very cumbersome, as it's only done in government labs, takes forever, and less than 0.1% of farmers in India actually do it. When farmers use fertilizer and pesticides they have no way of knowing if they are using the right amount. And this costs money.

The first step was to come up with a solution that could address this need. After researching alternatives, they came up with a prototype device like a dipstick that would allow a farmer to quickly gauge critical chemicals in their soil much like a blood sugar test for diabetes.

In addition to the technical details, their initial design targets looked to sell the gadget directly to the farmers. This constrained their solution in two ways. It required a product that had to be inexpensive as well as very easy to use as most of the farmers were not very literate.

Rethinking the business model with an alternative distribution and financial target can significantly change the requirements for the product making it more feasible. Since farmers do not have to test their soil frequently, the proposed device does not have to be really inexpensive. Instead looking at an alternative model that trains a local entrepreneur to provide soil testing services with this device, relaxes the constraints on their design significantly.

Since the entrepreneur will be able to recoup his costs and generate a healthy income by providing a service to hundreds of farmers, the cost target for the device could be raised several fold. In addition, these entrepreneurs, who are already trained by the Hubli Sandbox and ready to go, are more capable of handling sophisticated devices, further easing the requirements for design.

Working closely with local resources, like the Hubli Sandbox, to co-create appropriate and relevant solutions as well as the related business and implementation models ensures a much higher degree of success in social impact projects.

How do you measure real progress in a social enterprise?

Social entrepreneurs are definitely out to change people's lives for the better. And, they put in whatever it takes to make that dream come true.

You may be one of them.

How do you know if what you are doing is really working AND if you are making a meaningful difference?

Here is the litmus test for that.

If the work you are doing makes the people come back for more and you have a waiting list of potential beneficiaries, then you know you are having a meaningful impact.

In other words, there should be a pull from the target segment for a solution and not a push from you to embrace the solution.

Whenever possible try to get the people that are benefitting to share some of the value by paying for the solution. That will really show the hunger for the solution.

Even after you have asked for some money, if you still have a line of people waiting to be served, then you know you are onto something.

A word of caution.

It's easy to fall into a trap where you sugarcoat your offering to get people to buy into an intervention. You might see some initial traction, showcase progress, raise more funds, and continue sugarcoating the solution to get more people engaged.

This is the classic push approach and is unlikely to scale, let alone sustain itself.

As a social entrepreneur, one surefire way to see if you are having an impact is to see if the beneficiaries are willing to pay even a nominal amount to participate in the intervention.

Let's take an example from the farming sector in India.

Subsistence farmers need to increase their productivity and income and the biggest deciding factor is water. Access to water makes a huge difference in the amount they can produce.

There are simple hacks farmers can use to double or triple their productivity and income. One such hack is digging a farm pond, typically a 100x100x15 foot pit, that can be used to store rainwater to irrigate 5 acres of farm. We have implemented it recently in the Hubli Sandbox where we pay for part of the fixed costs and the farmers pay the variable costs. Because the return on their investment is so high, we have a huge line of people waiting for this intervention.

We know that we are making real progress in the farm pond project because of the wholehearted participation by the farmer and especially since they are willing to pay for it.

Having such a positive feedback loop provides you with a strong signal that you are making an impact. It helps you as it:

- Provides a financial model that you can use to scale up and impact more people

- Helps improve the intervention by getting feedback from those you serve. Since they pay, they receive the service with dignity and are not shy in voicing their opinion. This helps you to continuously improve the product similar to what you have to do in a competitive market segment.

 If the work you are doing makes the people come back for more and you have a waiting list of potential beneficiaries, then you know you are having a meaningful impact

Why capacity building is important in the social impact sector?

Capacity building is a necessary condition for you to succeed in the social impact sector. Unfortunately, this is not well understood and probably one of the main reasons for failure in this sector.

In for-profit entrepreneurship, the story is straightforward.

If you are serving people with disposable income. People will buy your product if you address a need that hasn't been fulfilled. The distribution channels are well developed. If it is a consumer product you can use channels like Amazon or Walmart to distribute the product. If you develop a product that meets a need, you have a winner in the making.

In the social impact sector, it is a different story.

You are trying to help those who are less fortunate, people who don't have disposable income. In fact, they may not be actively looking to spend their money on a solution.

For example, let's look at access to clean water.

There are enough benefits to using clean water that people should be motivated to buy it if you made it available for a few pennies a day. However, even a few pennies are precious for those who live on a few dollars a day.

Convincing people and getting them to buy into the value of clean water is not an easy task.

You need an economic model that provides an entrepreneur the opportunity to build a profitable business by convincing people of the benefits of clean drinking water and then selling it to them. To do so you need to both educate the entrepreneur about the opportunity as well as provide them with the tools to be successful. Even though their customers might be relatively poor, the entrepreneur can support him or herself by addressing the needs of hundreds of small consumers. As the entrepreneur is local, their own needs are typically modest and they might still make two or three times the income of their customers.

Ideas with positive impact can easily scale to reach millions by building such capacity in the field and by educating potential entrepreneurs.

What happens in most instances instead is that people come up with good solutions, but have no easy way to get it out to the people who need it. The missing link in the equation is the capacity-building infrastructure and the necessary new business models that will create a class of local entrepreneur to serve the people and disseminate the solution.

This takes time.

It takes time as you need to grow this capacity from within the community you are trying to serve. This involves identifying people who have the potential and hunger, but lack the education and support to grow as entrepreneurs.

Without this locally-grown capacity that acts as the distribution channel, the burden is on the entrepreneur or the organization to take their solution to the potential beneficiaries or customers at the bottom of the pyramid. It's nearly impossible to create a scalable, sustainable business model with this approach.

If your quest is to create long-term positive change, building capacity at the grassroots level should be your first step.

ENGAGE

How can successful professionals take part in social enterprises?

The world is filled with successful professionals.

They might be successful corporate executives or entrepreneurs who have done well.

People who've set aside enough money to take care of their needs, who don't have to work to pay their bills.

Increasingly these professionals are looking to use their talents and their time to make a bigger impact.

Their focus shifts from making money to making meaning; from achieving success to creating significance.

As they ponder their next step, they have a common question: **How and where can I get started on my social impact journey?**

The good news is that there are multiple ways for a successful professional to get involved.

It depends on how much of their time, energy, mindshare and money they are planning to set aside for the next phase of their life.

For example, they can join a social enterprise in any of the following roles, as:

- Donors or funders to fund the ecosystem that nurtures social entrepreneurs

- Board members to provide counsel and strategic direction

- Advisors to provide input and guidance using their key expertise

- Volunteers to help by contributing their time, talent and capabilities

- Full or part time employees in building an organization

Two highly successful social impact organizations - Agastya and Akshaya Patra – have tapped senior executives, including former CEOs of large corporations, to join their team. These executives have demonstrated the humility and desire to work at a non-profit and help people in need.

In my observation, I see that successful people who join social enterprises in their second innings are much happier than their contemporaries who might have attained success but are bored.

In their first innings, people are successful because they take risks, and solve problems.

They derive joy in solving big and complex problems.

Yet what can be more challenging than solving some of the trickiest social issues?

Many of our societal challenges are chronic, grand in scope and scale and, of course, very complex.

Attacking these challenging problems and trying to solve them is the best way for successful people to keep alive and vibrant.

If you are a successful professional who is getting bored, make sure you engage in one or more social impact projects and take on these big challenges. These organizations not only need your time, energy, money and mindshare, but also your vast experience from your successes in the corporate or entrepreneurial world.

Since the spectrum of involvement is wide, you can start anywhere from the sidelines as a supporter to an active role working at an organization or anywhere in between.

Whatever your choice, I can promise that it will be an enriching journey.

How do you attract top talent for your social enterprise?

Every enterprise, social or otherwise, needs awesome talent to create meaningful impact.

Early on in any enterprise, you typically don't have enough resources for pretty much anything. So, attracting great talent becomes a big challenge.

Under those circumstances, how do you attract the right talent to take your initiative to the next level?

For startups, it is most important to demonstrate your commitment and conviction to your mission and vision. Your potential employees need to see your conviction and commitment to the journey to the "promised land". By exciting them with that image you will attract the talent who share the common vision and commitment.

In addition, for for-profit startups, employees are willing to sacrifice short term salary for **greater potential future financial gains, making it easier to recruit.**

In social enterprises, employees are attracted to the mission and vision and their desire to make a significant and scalable social impact. The financial gains are secondary.

These passionate people are not running away from money, but are running towards meaning.

More than the for-profit sector, your ability to convey your vision of the change you are going to make in the world, is what will attract the most talented people to be a part of your mission. You might find these changemakers everywhere - at educational institutions where they are taking related courses, at relevant conferences, or as part of volunteering teams at relevant non-profits.

There is also another category of people who are looking for meaning after having made money.

Generally two things that motivate people are:

- The impact one can make on the world
- The financial gains from an endeavor

In the for-profit world, a large part of a person's decisions is driven by financial rewards. However there are a number of successful entrepreneurs and professionals who have achieved financial success and now are motivated primarily by their ability to use their time and resources to make a big difference in the world.

While the first phase of life might have been about money, for some the next phase is about making meaning. It's that group of people that has not been fully engaged. I see a lot of people who have had a successful career and are now looking for their second innings.

Social entrepreneurs who can tap into this demographic can find a valuable group of resources that they can get involved in many ways. These people not only bring extensive experience from successful for-profit ventures, but also are hungry to make meaning with their lives. It's the best of both worlds.

On engaging the general public to support your cause

In any project, engaging the stakeholders is not a trivial task.

It is an even harder task for social entrepreneurs.

In the for-profit world, you are trying to sell a product or a service to a customer. Getting the customer involved is the most important thing.

In the social impact sector, while you are typically trying to impact a particular segment of the society, your stakeholders and supporters might be from a different part of society. To succeed you need to get your stakeholders and supporters to understand and support your interventions.

You know your stakeholders are engaged when a significant number are connected to your project in whatever capacity.

For example, let's take Akshaya Patra.

Akshaya Patra is a midday meal program that provides food to over 1.4 million school children every day. Government subsidies for midday meals help cover 50% of the costs. The other 50% still needs to be raised from a whole bunch of people. By financially supporting the cause, people also get involved in spreading the message. This gets even more people involved and ultimately expands the impact of the program.

Getting broad-based support is very important, as it financially strengthens the organization by making it less dependent on one or two significant donors. It also creates a groundswell of support promoting the organization that in turn multiplies the impact.

Another example from the Sandbox is the Navodyami program.

The Navodyami program aims to help small business people become better entrepreneurs. Most of them don't have a formal education, but are skilled at solving problems and making the most with very little. They could benefit greatly from a program like a MBA 101, which would give them some basic business skills.

In the Sandbox, we have several successful businesses with annual revenues of around 2 to 5 crore rupees. They may not be considered big businesses, but would make great mentors for the small business entrepreneurs that come to Navodyami.

When we engage these successful business people to help out the Navodyami micro-entrepreneurs, the impact is just amazing.

Everybody in society has something to give, even if they aren't the most accomplished business people. They need to be just successful enough to help someone who was like them ten years ago.

This is good for two different reasons:

- It leverages the manpower we have in society to help others

- It brings joy, pride, and identity to those who participate in the mentoring and giving back

In the for-profit world, a typical entrepreneur raises money from family, friends, angels and VCs. These people take different levels of risk and help the entrepreneur in hopes that their own money will grow.

In the social impact sector, one needs a lot of resources to have meaningful impact. Entrepreneurs need to be more creative because they can't get everything from one type of supporter. They need to be master storytellers to gain support and get resources from people who might have a connection to the social mission or the segment of society that the entrepreneur aims to serve.

In summary, the greater the public engagement, the better the chances of a large impact.

About Desh Deshpande

Gururaj "Desh" Deshpande is a Trustee of Deshpande Foundation along with his wife Jaishree. Desh is also the President and Chairman of Sparta Group LLC, a family investment office.

Dr. Deshpande has pursued an entrepreneurial career and built several companies including Cascade Communications and Sycamore Networks.

Dr. Deshpande lives in Boston and serves as a life-member of the MIT Corporation.

Deshpande Foundation set up MIT's Deshpande Center for Technological Innovation, Deshpande Center for Social Entrepreneurship in India, Entrepreneurship for All (EforAll) in Lowell/Lawrence Massachusetts and Pond-Deshpande Center at the University of New Brunswick in Canada. They were founding funders of UPOP at MIT, I-Corp at NSF and MassChallenge.

Dr. Deshpande holds a B. Tech. in Electrical Engineering from the Indian Institute of Technology - Madras, an M.E. from the University of New Brunswick in Canada, and Ph.D from Queen's University in Canada.

Deshpande co-chaired a National Council to support President Obama's innovation and entrepreneurship strategy.